Table of Contents

Introduction

Thank you for choosing my book; Greenhouse Gardening for Beginners: The ultimate guide on how to build a greenhouse and grow vegetables, fruits and herbs all year round. This ultimate guide will inform you on all you need to know to start growing vegetables, edible flowers and herbs in a greenhouse garden.

Gardening is a simple term that refers to the science of soil cultivation on a small or large scale for food production or for ornamental purposes. When a plant is cultivated outdoors without an enclosure, the growth rate of such a plant depends on the climatic condition provided by nature. This makes it possible to produce such a plant only within its growing season. If you desire to extend the natural growing season of a certain plant or in other words, make the plant available out of season, the technology to employ is the greenhouse technology. Greenhouse gardening is not exactly a new technology, because it has been in existence as far back as the 13th century. It is purposely used to ensure continuous productivity of plants. In certain areas of the world where there is adverse climatic condition and the soil is unfit for plant cultivation, alternative solutions have been sorted and employed over the years to ensure successful plant cultivation. Among these alternative solutions is the greenhouse technology which advertently protects the plant from unfavorable environmental conditions (such as excessive heat, cold, pests and diseases, etc.) and therefore ensures plant's healthy growth.

The purpose of this guide is to help you understand and get the basic knowledge of greenhouse gardening, its maintenance and all that is required for optimum productivity at the end of the growing season. In all hopes, this guide will simplify everything about greenhouse gardening such that it becomes an easy practice.

Chapter 1: What to consider before buying a greenhouse

Mini greenhouse buyer's guide

Location:

This is the most important point, and the one that you must start with. Nothing is better than finding a place that has an abundance of light and is well protected from strong winds. Getting things right at the beginning prevents you from unnecessary hassle and expense in the future. Choose a site that has limited shade and a smaller number of trees nearby. This is because falling leaves and branches may harm your greenhouse and will also prevent valuable sunlight from reaching your plants. Alternately, you can install heating units in the greenhouse. However, avoid using low quality heaters that will multiply your electricity bill. Make sure there is at least two feet of access space around for cleaning or other activities.

Heating:

If you are planning to raise seeds in the winter then you may need extra heat. In contrast, the summer can be a better option for you as you may have a favorable climate to work with. You can use gas or you can burn wood to heat up the internal environment, as installing an electricity supply may be very expensive.

Dimensions:

A greenhouse should have dimensions that are at least six feet wide. However, you can also extend the space later if required. Frames should be made of wood or aluminum. Using a plain aluminum body can save you money initially. If you can get them, color-coated aluminum can also be of use. Half-bordered framing is cheaper to use than covering the whole floor to ceiling with complete glass.

Venting:

In order to provide good growing conditions, the glazing must have vents. The combined area of vents must be at least a fifth of the total floor area. Venting invites fresh air and additional sunlight.

Roof shape:

A proper roof shape is essential for an effective greenhouse. A curved or angled side allows more light to get in.

Height:

The greenhouse should leave at least one foot of space above your head when standing. If you are growing slightly taller plants like cordon tomatoes then your greenhouse needs to have a minimum of 5 feet of space from the base to the eaves.

Door design:

The hinged doors used in the greenhouse should have a strong grip to hold them open or closed. You can also use a sliding door. Adding a metal kick panel at the base will limit the likelihood of damage. Make sure the dimensions of the doors will provide you with enough space to get in or to carry plants through.

Staging:

You can make shelving for plants with timber or aluminum. However, using a second-hand aluminum staging setup is always a cheaper option.

Water management:

Provide an adequate drainage system so the unused water passes away easily without creating any pooling in the greenhouse. Also, ensure that you have a sufficient water source close to the greenhouse for watering.

Chapter 2: Constructing a greenhouse

All about how to build a homemade greenhouse

Start by choosing a location. Greenhouses require lots of sunlight. Choose a spot that gives you adequate sunlight. This is usually found on the southern side of any garden or farmland. It is important to choose the spot that gives maximum morning sun and is not obstructed by tall plants or trees. This will reduce the amount of sunlight that the greenhouse will receive. Another important thing to remember while choosing the spot for the greenhouse is the other structures in the periphery of the greenhouse. All of these structures are best located on the northern side of the garden or farmland.

Measure your location using a tape and remember the bigger your greenhouse is, the more money you will require to make it. If you have little to no experience in building things, then it is best to get a greenhouse kit that will give you all the materials that you will require.

The best locations are the ones that are constructed with one wall that is already built. In this way, you can use this one wall to construct the remaining portion of your greenhouse. Also, if the wall is that of your house, the warmth will be an additional boost to the plants in the greenhouse. Support this structure with wooden beams or steel beams or rebar.

Build a frame using the support structures as a guide. The easiest is to create a dome-shaped greenhouse. However, the problem is the lack of space inside. Create and build frames using steel beams and connect these dome beams using steel rods or wooden rods. It is very important to choose a sturdy and rigid frame. It is best to seek architectural help to prevent the frames from toppling over.

Once the skeletal system for the greenhouse is built you can start by choosing the material you want over the greenhouse. Unless you are a professional who has had lots of prior experience, it is best to stick with a cover that is sturdy and functional. Specialized plastic and covers like UV stabilized polyethylene are good alternate sources. They are durable, light, and inexpensive. They also allow a good quantity of light transmission. The downside is that they need replacement and require washing as they accumulate dust and won't be as effective as glass. Alternately you can use a double walled plastic called polycarbonate or fiberglass, which are slightly more expensive materials but still excellent alternates.

Connect the entire area with dowels and a good hardy wire and place stakes on the ground. Add a layer of rebar for additional reinforcement. You can also add PVC if you want.

Once the PVC and rebar set, pour a good quantity of gravel inside the boundaries. This will act as a drainage for the plants and will absorb excess water, keeping the soil moist. It is also advisable to pour concrete on the floor of the greenhouse.

Get good quality wood and ensure you treat it to avoid degradation and depreciation. Cut and mold to fill the ground of the greenhouse by accounting for the way you want the plants to be arranged and the area available for plants, and to build any segregating units.

It is best to use metal dowels to keep the wooden drafts and segregation around. This will strengthen the pieces and account for less wear and tear and damage.

Seal the covering to the frame and ensure this is done as close to the frame as possible. You can tape and nail the material of the cover to the wooden frame. But take note to not stretch the material too much as this could tear the material. It is advisable to take your time doing this step.

Next comes the plan to control the environment of the greenhouse. Get heaters and fans to generate heat during the entire winter seasons. Place them in four corners in a diagonal position to account for optimal heating. Be sure to run these the entire winter to allow the plants to get the required warmth. It is also a good idea to install vents on the roof of the greenhouse, if this is not possible, build windows at the upper side of the walls to prevent the air from getting stale inside and to also prevent excess heat. These vents will also allow you to reduce the amount of carbon dioxide inside the greenhouse.

Install perforated pipes along the areas where the plants are going to be cultivated inside the greenhouse. This will account for good irrigation. You can also construct the cultivable area of the land in a raised sloping platform to prevent excess water retention. It is also a good idea to have a couple of thermometers to measure the temperature of the environment inside the greenhouse and planting those plants, which are suitable for that particular temperature.

Chapter 3: Building elements

Location

The location of your greenhouse also depends on many factors. The first factor is the type of plant you want to grow inside your greenhouse. Tropical plants need a maximum sunlight exposure so you must choose a greenhouse where sunlight comes in appropriate amount. Most houseplants and flowers need a good exposure to sunlight but not direct. Your location also depends on the climate of your area. If you live in a warm place, then you must need proper shading for your greenhouse. However, if you live in cold area then you need maximum exposure of sunlight. Remember that sun changes its position in different seasons. A very sunny spot in June should not get any sun exposure during January season and you must consider this fact before choosing your greenhouse location.

Floor

You have a choice what kind of floor or base you want for your greenhouse. Many people don't bother to cover their greenhouse base and they generally have mud or other floor where they constructed their greenhouse. This gives a natural look to your greenhouse. But it is not advisable to keep your floor open because many insects, worms, and rodents may grow inside the mud and should harm your plants. Some base constructions are available with the greenhouse construction kit and you don't need to buy extra material for your base. But if it is not available in your kit, you can buy it from the market. Concrete floors are the good option for your greenhouse's base as they make the best place to put your benches and other materials. Sometimes, wooden floors are also good for your greenhouse

Foundation

When you are building a greenhouse, the first step is to build a foundation. This needs to be done properly for you to have a solid greenhouse that will stand the test of time.

Whatever you decide to make your foundation out of, it needs to be both level and square. It needs to be big enough for the outside dimensions of the greenhouse to ensure it fits properly and can be secured.

You can buy pre-made greenhouse bases, and these are worth considering, but just be aware that these still need a flat and level surface to be installed on and will still need a foundation beneath them.

When building your greenhouse base, you can either make it out of poured concrete, or you can use sand and paving stones. Both are suitable and do the job well, though the latter has the advantage of being moveable in the future if necessary.

Ensure that not only are the edges of your base square but also that the diagonal measurements between the corners are also identical.

Under the base, you will need the foundation which is what supports the weight of the greenhouse, which it is secured to and prevents damage in windy weather.

If you live in an area where the ground freezes then your greenhouse foundation needs to be below the frost line. This is to prevent damage to your structure from the ground heaving as it freezes and melts. Your local Building Permit Agency will be able to tell you where the frost line is in your area. In warmer areas, this is only going to be a couple of inches at most, but in the colder, northern areas it can be as much as a few feet.

One good way of insulating your foundation and protecting it is to use 1" foam insulation. Put this down to your frost line to reduce heat loss through the soil, which has the benefit of reducing your heating costs.

The foundation is essential because this is what you are securing your greenhouse too. It will prevent weather damage and warping in hot or cold weather. If you do not secure your greenhouse properly, then don't expect it to last the growing season. If the greenhouse starts to warp, then you can find your panes shatter or crack and become very hard to re-fit. You can also find doors and windows become stiff and very difficult to use too.

If you have bought a new greenhouse, then any warranty will not cover damage due to not having a proper greenhouse base.

Your greenhouse is built on this foundation and base, which will ensure it is easier to erect and that it will last.

There are some different choices for the foundation, which we'll discuss now.

Compacted Soil

If you compact the soil enough, then you can build your greenhouse directly on the ground, particularly if you live in an area where the ground doesn't freeze too badly.

A lot of greenhouses will come with an optional metal plinth which has spikes in each corner. These can be cemented into the ground to prevent the base from moving.

You will still need to level the ground though, so dig out your spirit level. It is best to use a roller or other mechanical device to compact the soil to ensure it is stable. Do not build your base out of gravel or hardcore because these are just not stable enough.

The advantage of using the soil as your foundation is that it is very cost effective. You can also use the existing ground for growing your plants in plus drainage is a lot better.

The downside of soil is that it will allow pests into your greenhouse. You will find this particularly bad in winter as pests flock to your greenhouse for the warmth.

Perimeter Bases

This is a slightly cheaper option where you use either bricks, breeze blocks or thin paving or edging slabs to create a foundation directly under the greenhouse frame. You can use concrete if you prefer.

The foundation is built along where the frame will run, leaving the soil in the middle of the greenhouse untouched.

While you can build the foundation directly on the soil, most people will cut out a trench and place the foundation in the trench. The advantage of this latter approach is that it is easier to level.

Slabs or Paving

This is a very popular way to build your greenhouse foundation because it keeps out the weeds and pests while giving you a good, clean growing environment.

This method involves building a base the size of your greenhouse out of paving slabs and then fixing your greenhouse to it. This type of base will last for many years and is very low maintenance.

You can screw your greenhouse to the base to provide stability in windy conditions, preventing any damage. It also provides good drainage when compared to an all concrete base.

In the winter months, a soil floor can get damp and encourage mold to grow. A paved floor helps to keep the greenhouse both warmer and drier in the cooler months.

Providing you bed down the slabs properly with an inch or two of sand underneath them they are surprisingly easy to get level and will not warp or move over time.

Concrete Base

This is where you mark out where your greenhouse will be and dig down a few inches before pouring concrete in to form the base.

For larger greenhouses, this has its advantages, but it can be expensive and does require specialist tools such as a concrete mixer.

This is a very durable base, and you can fit expansion bolts to secure larger structures. You may have an issue with standing water so may want to consider putting drainage holes in to prevent standing water.

Frame

The frame is extremely important, because it provides the integrity of the structure, and also anchors the greenhouse covering.

The materials available for frames are:

Aluminum

This will provide a very strong frame that does not rust, and it's lightweight. It has a very long lifespan and it's the most widely used frame for greenhouses. Aluminum has extruding channels, which are perfect for inserting the covering panels.

Steel

Steel that is galvanized is very strong and long lasting plus, it's reasonably priced. Because of its strength, you require just a little for the framing, which adds the amount of light passing on to the plants.

Steel is also very heavy and ensures the greenhouse remains solid no matter the weather conditions or temperature levels. However, the transportation and assembling of the greenhouse can be difficult since the steel is heavy.

Plastic Resin

These are very attractive, and are very popular. This is because, compared to aluminum, they are less expensive, and they also do not conduct any heat away from the greenhouse like steel does.

Unfortunately, they lack the strength of the metal frames, and can only be used for the smaller greenhouses, with shorter dimensions. They can only be used with the polycarbonate panels.

Wood

Wooden frames are ideal for a simple do-it-yourself greenhouse project. Wood is beautiful in appearance and provides sufficient durability and strength but it is susceptible to rotting, therefore don't allow contact with moisture.

Tempered Glass

These are strong and impact-resistant. This means that they will withstand any expansions or contractions during the seasonal temperature changes. The 3mm single pane thickness is ideal for the greenhouse.

However, the 4mm thickness is much stronger and will provide additional insulation. You must protect the hedges during insulation, as the glass may shatter if hit hard. Tempered glass is much more expensive compared to the polycarbonate panels.

Tempered glass is more durable even if it's expensive, and it is more resistant to scratches, as well as being very clear and providing no diffusion.

Fiberglass

This is translucent and provides a light that is well-diffused. Fiberglass retains heat better than normal glass. The greenhouses made from fiberglass are normally corrugated to provide adequate rigidity because the outer coat will become sunbaked within 6-10 years. The surface will become etched and yellow.

Polycarbonate

It is UV treated, lightweight and durable. It is a high quality and modern material used for greenhouses. The polycarbonate is available in different levels of thickness and provides the clarity of glass, but it's not scratch resistant, or as strong as the tempered glass.

The single-walled one does not retain any heat and provides no light diffusion. It, however, has a longer lifespan of more than 15 years, depending on the region.

Twin-Walled Polycarbonate

This is very popular because it has internal spaces providing strength and excellent insulation. The best point to note about the twin-walled polycarbonate is that it diffuses light.

Triple-Walled Polycarbonate

This is similar to twin-walled polycarbonate, but it has extra strength and heat retention abilities. In cold climates, the triple-walled polycarbonate is extremely useful for an all-year-round indoor gardening, because it will withstand snow loads and will freeze without cracking or distorting.

Wind securities

Any surface such as a wall, fence, or even nearby buildings can act as protection against gusts of wind or even snow. When plants are close to these surfaces, they can leech onto the small amount of warmth that they provide. During summer, if your plants cannot stand the heat, you can use these surfaces as sun blocks.

Chapter 4: Greenhouse environment

Heat

If the winters in your area are on the harsh side, or if you want to get a head start on seed germination before spring, you will need to consider adding in heating for your greenhouse.

Electrical heaters today are a lot more energy efficient than they used to be. The most important thing when it comes to choosing your heater is that it should have a thermostat – this helps to keep the temperature constant and makes the whole system more energy-efficient as the heater is turned off when the desired temperature has been reached.

There are several different types of heaters that you can get that are suited to greenhouses. Tubular heaters, fan heaters, and warming cables are all options to consider.

I do advise getting in a qualified electrician to help install the heating system because the plugs, etc. need to be waterproofed due to the high levels of humidity in the room.

Shade

The sun in summer can really scorch your plants, especially in a greenhouse.

It is advisable to have shades fitted to the outside that can be easily rolled into place as necessary.

Ventilation

Without proper ventilation and air circulation, your plants are more vulnerable to attack by fungus and mold. You should only cut off the air supply in the very coldest of weather.

Air circulation helps to keep the temperature in the room constant in summer and prevents your plants from being stifled.

The general rule is that you need at least two ventilators for every 6 feet in length.

Having ventilators on both sides of the greenhouse allows you to choose the better option when it comes to cutting out howling wind.

Ventilators come in many forms. Louver windows are popular and good for creating airflow but make sure that they are tight-fitting when closed so as not to allow drafts in.

Humidity

Humidity here refers to the amount of moisture in the greenhouse growing environment. It is no news that keeping the wrong humidity in the greenhouse is detrimental to the growth of the plants. Here are a few tips on how to maintain the right relative humidity:

1. Avoid overwatering your growing medium. Too much watering is the beginning of trouble in the plants' root system. The humidity level in the greenhouse increases when there is too much water in the medium.

2. Ensure enough air circulation. This will improve the ventilation in the greenhouse and invariably ensure the right humidity level.

Lighting

While your electrician is fitting the heaters, it makes sense for them to also fit lights for the greenhouse. The type of light will depend on what the purpose of the light is.

You can make the space more aesthetically appealing by spotlighting particular areas in the greenhouse or more practical by adding in strip lighting.

Again, you should not place the lights too close to the actual plants. A ultra-violet lamp can also be installed to provide better lighting in low-light conditions.

LED lighting is more expensive to install upfront but a lot more energy efficient than the incandescent bulbs or even your energy-saver bulbs.

It is also a good idea to place the light switches close to the entrance of the greenhouse so that you can find them easily in the dark.

Irrigation

If your greenhouse is in your garden then it is easy enough to pop down and water it, but if it is at an allotment or you are on holiday then watering becomes much trickier, putting your harvest at risk.

In the hottest weather, and more so in hotter climates, you will need to water your plants two or three times a day to keep them healthy no matter how good your cooling system is!

Although you can hand water the plants in your greenhouse, this can soon get boring and difficult to keep up. The best and most efficient way to water your plants is to invest in a greenhouse irrigation system. Which you choose will depend on the size of your greenhouse, what you are growing and whether or not you have electricity and water to hand.

If you are planning to irrigate your greenhouse, then the need to be sited near to water and/or electricity can heavily influence your choice of location.

There are a lot of different irrigation systems on the market with widely varying prices, so you do need to spend some time considering your requirements before rushing out to buy one.

Some plants require more water than others, so depending on what you are growing you may want to get an automatic irrigation system that can deliver differing quantities of water to different plants.

You also want a system that can grow with you as you put more plants in your greenhouse. At certain times within the season you will have more plants in your greenhouse than at others, so your irrigation system needs to be able to support this extra demand.

You do need to be careful because any irrigation system that is introducing too much water to your greenhouse could end up making it too damp, which will encourage the growth of diseases. This is one reason why you need to have your drainage and ventilation right to prevent damage to your greenhouse ecosystem.

Chapter 5: Greenhouse VS polytunnel

In many ways, a polytunnel is very similar to a greenhouse in that it insulates your plants from the weather and helps them thrive.

Polytunnels are typically made from plastic or aluminum pipes and covered with a strong plastic sheeting.

These are much cheaper than greenhouses, but they aren't quite the same.

A polytunnel is much weaker than a greenhouse and more likely to be damaged in high winds. It also does not provide the same level of insulation as a greenhouse. It is still excellent for growing plants and keeping them warm, but in the colder months, it will be harder to heat and keep warm.

A lot of serious growers will start their plants off in a greenhouse before moving them into a polytunnel to complete their growing season. Frost tender plants are then often moved back into the greenhouse in winter for that extra protection from the weather.

A polytunnel is a good starter for growing with many similar considerations to a greenhouse. Remember to buy the strongest you can afford and secure it against the wind fully.

Chapter 6: What to grow in a polytunnel and greenhouse

What to grow in a greenhouse?

Choosing your plants for greenhouse gardening is a very crucial step. There are a lot of plants and vegetable to choose from. When you are new at greenhouse gardening, then you must be able to start with those that are easy to grow and maintain so as time goes by, you can learn to deal with the complicated ones at any time during the year.

Leafy greens

These are very common among greenhouse gardeners. It is also an unwritten rule to always start with anything that belongs in the salad family which is almost all the leafy vegetables or greens. Not only are they easy to grow, they can also be a great source of income.

Spinach

Considered to be one of the most grown greenhouse gardening plants. To be able to enjoy the freshest piece of spinach, pick one right from your greenhouse then cook it immediately. That way, it would both be very tasty and healthy.

Tomatoes

Tomatoes are known to be very low maintenance in a greenhouse. That is why they are very easy to grow and maintain, especially those in the beefsteak family.

Herbs

Planted with or without roots, herbs are great with either. Plus, it is perfect for an indoor greenhouse garden.

Citrus fruits

winter fruits can grow just right inside your greenhouse like sweet and sour, delicious looking melons, oranges and lemons.

What to grow in a polytunnel?

French beans,Peppers, Chillies, Basil, Scallions Courgettes, Cucumbers, Melons, Sweetcorn, Coriander, Dill and Chervil, , Aubergines Lettuce, Pak choi, Parsley, , Chinese cabbage, Florence fennel

Chapter 7: How to efficiently heat and cool a greenhouse

Heating a greenhouse

An unheated (cold) greenhouse is generally a protected spot to grow more tender crops such as tomatoes and cucumbers in the summer, mums in the fall, and not much use in winter except to over-winter very hardy plants through the colder months.

If you want to extend your growing season and the range of plants you can grow, you'll need some way to heat your greenhouse during colder months. If you've decided on a cool greenhouse, the most common type for home gardeners, then maintain temperatures above 45 degrees F.

Electric heat is the best choice – no fumes and easily controlled. Hire a professional to install any electric heaters. Electric fan heaters are the most common - and best - choice for a small greenhouse. They circulate the air quickly, and some will allow the fan to run even when the heating element is switched off.

Electric heating cables are another option. The most common is the soil heating type, placed in the soil or on staging under the plants. This is a very economical heating method, since you're directing heat exactly where it's required.

Another choice is a fuel stove – wood, natural gas, propane or paraffin. These all require adequate ventilation, and control of the heat is not easy, except in the case of gases.

The only recommended type of fuel is propane, with the bottles placed on a flat firm surface outside the greenhouse. Water vapor and carbon dioxide are both produced as a burn by-product. Be aware that too much water vapor can cause mold to grow.

If you've opted for a lean-to attached to your house or a conservatory/sun room, tap into your in-house heating. However, you'll need a separate thermostat, since house heating may be set too low at night, just when the greenhouse requires added heat.

Cooling a greenhouse

The temperature inside a cool greenhouse is generally kept above 45 degrees Fahrenheit (7 degrees Celsius). Both heat and light require supplementing during the cool months. The plants inside are protected from wind, rain, snow and frost.

In a cool greenhouse, you can grow a larger variety of plants, perhaps as many as you would in an outdoor garden.

Growth here is 3 to 4 weeks ahead of a cold greenhouse. This is a great place to start less hardy bedding plants, and to over-winter frost-sensitive perennials.

Chapter 8: Greenhouse heating, cooling and ventilation process in the details

Heating

In the greenhouse, both heat and light come primarily from the sun. This is particularly true of the hobby greenhouse. A commercial rose grower may have to spend thousands of dollars a week on oil heat in January to get his product ready for the all-important Valentine's Day season, but most of us greenhouses derive 90 percent or more of the light and heat used for growing our plants from the sun.

Solar heat

Your greenhouse should be well designed to maximize the production of solar heat within the building and minimize heat loss at night or on cloudy days. For a discussion of glazing materials, placement of glazed areas, insulation, and caulking, see Greenhouse Basics: Building Your Own Greenhouse.

Preventing Overheating

Heat in a greenhouse is similar to water in this regard: It is more likely that plants will be injured by too much of it than by too little. Any greenhouse, but in particular one that has roof as well as wall glazing, can overheat in the spring and summer months, from April to September. Unless precautions are taken, it is not unusual for temperatures inside such a building to rise to well above 120 degrees, which is hot enough to kill some plants and injure others severely.

There are two ways to prevent overheating. One is to reduce the amount of glazed area; the other, more common, practice is through ventilation. In earlier times, the standard method of reducing the glazed area for a commercial greenhouse, one that is still in use to some extent, was whitewashing. In late spring or early summer, a white compound was sprayed on the exterior of the glass. This material was so designed that a succession of summer rains washed it off; ideally, enough of it was gone by October that it did not need to be removed manually.

Whitewash doesn't work well on glazing materials other than glass, and most hobby greenhouse owners, even those who use glass, don't trouble with it. Instead, they, like the majority of commercial greenhouse owners, cover the top glazed surfaces with shade cloth. This is reasonably inexpensive and lasts several seasons. It is not difficult to apply on freestanding greenhouses, although it may be a pain to work with on attached greenhouses that have a few skylights or an entire glass roof. Some arrangement with inexpensive plastic tarpaulins may have to be worked out for such structures.

Heating in winter

After working all summer to keep the greenhouse cool, the poor greenhouser must work all winter to keep it warm. Rarely will the sun alone suffice. Some artificial heat is necessary, not so much on the coldest days as on the cloudiest ones, and of course at night.

A well-designed attached greenhouse with sufficient insulation and heat-sink material will not need much supplemental heat. If, in addition, there is a system of shutters to cover the glazed area at night, it will need very little. But it will still need some. This supplemental heat can probably be obtained from the house, either through openings or simply by leakage through the wall and glass doors. (It is not only unnecessary but also unwise to insulate the wall between the greenhouse and the house.)

Whether additional heat will be needed depends not only on the construction of the greenhouse, but also on what use you make of it in the coldest, darkest months. If nothing is grown, or if only cold-hardy plants like lettuce and radishes are cultivated, less heat will be needed than if tomatoes or African violets are being grown.

If the plants need more warmth than can be obtained by simply allowing heat from the house to flow into the greenhouse, or if the design makes that impossible, then some nonsolar heat source is necessary. Most artificial heat comes from combustion—that is, from burning fuels like coal, wood, or gas. Combustion gives off gases, many of which are harmful to plants as well as to people.

Electric Heat

The best heating arrangement for a greenhouse involves having the combustion take place elsewhere. Basically, this is what electric heat does, the combustion usually taking place hundreds of miles away or not at all, as when the electricity is generated by water power or nuclear fission. The best heat for a greenhouse or any other building is electric heat, except for one small problem: In most parts of the United States and Canada, it costs much more per unit of heat than burning wood, gas, oil, or coal.

If you need only a small amount of artificial heat for your greenhouse, then it is certainly best to use electricity, in one of three ways. The first, most extensive, and most expensive method is to install one or more electric baseboard heaters. The fact that your greenhouse probably doesn't have baseboards needn't deter you; baseboard heaters don't require baseboards. Such heaters are relatively inexpensive and easy to install. You can do it yourself if you're handy and the local building code permits.

The second method is a small, self-contained radiator. The smallest of these are on wheels so that they may be placed where the need is greatest. They sometimes are filled with water, but more often with oil, which has certain advantages, one being that it won't freeze and burst the radiator as readily as water. They can be plugged into any outlet and include a thermostat, so that they can be set to turn themselves on and off at the greenhouser's discretion. These are extremely popular with small hobby greenhousers.

The third method is the most common and is often used in conjunction with other heat sources. It is a soil or flat heater. In most cases, particularly with sprouting seeds, it is not the air temperature, but the soil temperature, that is crucial. Most garden supply houses stock several kinds of these heaters, and many seed catalogs offer them.

Ventilation

Air circulation is very important in the greenhouse as it ensures that the required temperature is maintained. The amount of air to be supplied per time in the greenhouse depends on the size of the greenhouse, the type of plant cultivated, and also the climatic condition of the area where the greenhouse is set up. The equipment installed for supplying air in the greenhouse should be sufficient for the entire plantation.

The greenhouse environment created for the plants being cultivated is of utmost importance. It is the greenhouse environment that dictates the condition of plant growth. However big or small the greenhouse is, the environmental condition created is what determines the successful cultivation of the plants in the system. This means that you should pay more attention to creating the right greenhouse environment.

Cooling

While ensuring the right growing environment in a greenhouse, the elements can be controlled manually, automatically or through an integrated control system. The integrated control system uses several sensors and computer systems in the greenhouse such that the soil temperature, humidity, air level, and light level are sensed and then controlled as required. In order to maintain the right growing temperature in your greenhouse, the type of temperature control system chosen matters. You should consider the cost of installation and maintenance of the control equipment and ensure that the equipment is able to maintain uniform temperature by regulating extreme temperatures to enhance plant growth. You should also avoid power outages in the greenhouse by putting a backup generator in place in case of power failure at any time. You should also pay attention to the ways through which heat is lost in the greenhouse and replenish them in order to keep the greenhouse warm at the right temperature.

How to Maintain the right Temperature in the Greenhouse

Regardless of the size of your greenhouse, the system temperature is one of the important factors that determine successful cultivation. Below are tips on how to maintain the right greenhouse temperature:

1. Install sensors or better yet, monitoring system in your greenhouse. This will help to monitor the change in temperature of your greenhouse. Some sensors will also give feedback on the moisture level of your greenhouse.

2. Ensure sufficient ventilation. The enclosed greenhouse can sometimes create a heated growing environment, sufficient ventilation is then needed to keep the right temperature range. Install cooling systems such as fans or air conditioners depending on your greenhouse size and plant type.

3. Pay attention to your lighting in the system. Depending on the

external weather condition, adjust your greenhouse lighting accordingly to maintain the right temperature. Install grow lights if necessary and you may also want to consider installing heaters.

Chapter 9: Factors that affect heat loss

Conduction

This is the main way through which heat is lost. Movement of air is responsible convection of heat to the inside surface of the greenhouse. Movement of air outside is what causes convection of heat away from the outside.

Air exchange

The movement of warm air from the greenhouse to outside and movement of cold air from outside of the greenhouse is also another factor affecting the heat loss in the greenhouse.

Air infiltration

This usually depends on the type, age and condition in which a greenhouse is in. Greenhouses that are in poor condition usually have some cracks near the doors or have holes in material covering where so much cold air enters from and in large quantities. Those greenhouses that are covered with fiberglass in large sheets, or glazing materials have little or no infiltration.

Chapter 10: How to irrigate your greenhouse to reduce the amount of plant loss caused by stress induced by delivering an inconsistent amount of water or fertilizer

Drip Irrigation

One of the best forms of irrigation is drip irrigation. Not only do you get to save a lot of water through this method (you can waste more than 40% water using a sprinkler system), but you can also prevent your leaves from getting wet, which could potentially attract diseases in the future.

However, I know that you cannot completely avoid using sprinklers, as it all depend on how you would like to grow your garden. If you have to use sprinklers, then I recommend timing your sprinkler system. Once you spray water on the plants, let the leaves dry before sprinkling water on them again.

Watering

Watering of plants regularly within a greenhouse is not compulsory as the structure itself builds up its humidity system. You are only required to water once the soil is dry. Nevertheless, plants needs are varied, and some plants require more water than others particularly in the hot season. It is necessary to measure the humidity and moisture with a moisture gauge within the greenhouse. Whether you choose to water by a misting system, drip irrigation or hand, keep a journal of when to water specific plants and maintain that routine.

Watering is of the utmost importance when it comes to running a successful greenhouse. But watering cannot be a haphazard affair and there must be some measure of consistency in it in order for you to be able to make the most use of your produce. Most veggies for example will not grow the biggest and develop the best hues unless you are consistent with their watering. Without consistency what should be otherwise big, juicy red tomatoes will end up being scrawny and splotchy green and red, dried up cherries. So just show some consistency and all the rest will follow.

Overhead Misters

If you grow mostly or all one type of plant, then an overhead watering method is a great choice because you can water all your plants evenly and easily. For larger greenhouses, this is a great system because it will water a large area quickly.

The downside of this type of system is that it is quite wasteful of water because the water goes everywhere in the greenhouse, not just into the containers where your plants are.

Your plants end up getting a lot of water on their leaves. If they are over-crowded or ventilation is poor, then this can cause problems such as powdery mildew and make your plants more susceptible to disease.

Mat Irrigation

You can buy capillary matting which works as an irrigation system for your plants. This is a special mat that is designed to draw up water which is then absorbed by your plants through moisture wicks which go into the soil of your containers.

The mat is kept moist by a drip watering system, so you do not have to run water piping throughout your greenhouse. It can just go to strategic points where it feeds the capillary matting.

This is a relatively cheap method of irrigation and is very simple to install. The big advantage is it is very efficient in its use of water, and there is little risk of overwatering your plants!

Chapter 11: How to avoid wind damage for your greenhouse

One of the biggest dangers your greenhouse faces is the wind. A high wind can rip a greenhouse to pieces, twisting the frame and shattering the glass, so you need to take steps to protect your precious greenhouse and the plants inside.

Firstly, you need to make sure that all the panes of glass are securely in place and none are broken. A corner missing out of a pane can give the wind ingress to then blow out other panes and damage your greenhouse. Although a greenhouse isn't a completely sealed unit, solid panes will help to protect it from wind damage.

You can buy a galvanized steel base for your greenhouse, which usually comes as a flat pack. Although not essential these are extremely helpful as the base will raise up your greenhouse a little and helps make it more stable because you can secure the base to the foundation and the greenhouse to the base.

A greenhouse base is secured to the foundation by pushing specially designed metal hooks into pockets of wet concrete which are then secured to the frame. An alternative fixing is to lay a concrete strip that sits under the greenhouse base. Drilling then secures the base as it is bolted it to the concrete.

One of the favorite ways to secure a greenhouse is to lay a single course of bricks on a concrete footing and then secure the greenhouse to the bricks without using a greenhouse base. In some cases, you may want to use wooden batons between the greenhouse and the bricks.

Of course, you can dramatically reduce the potential for damage simply by locating your greenhouse in a more sheltered area. The trouble is you often have to balance sun exposure with shelter, but you will have to make that judgment call based on your knowledge of your site.

Although you can do everything possible to protect your greenhouse, no matter what you do you cannot make it complete stormproof. There will also be cases where a freak storm hits. If severe weather warnings are given for your area, then you should probably remove any plants you want to save to another location where they will be protected during the storm.

If your greenhouse is square and level, then it is more likely to have better fitting glass. Loose glass will rattle, and this has much more chance of breaking. The gaps in a non-square frame allows the wind into the greenhouse where it can cause all sorts of destruction.

Most greenhouses will have a flexible rubber glazing seal between the glass and the aluminum frame. These have a tendency to perish over time and will frequently disappear when moving a greenhouse. These seals hold the glass in place and prevents the wind getting into your greenhouse. Regularly check your seals and replace them if they start to perish. It will go a long way to protecting your greenhouse from wind damage.

Glazing clips hold the glass to the frame, and these have a habit of vanishing. They pop off during wind storms, get knocked off and generally vanish. You should check the glazing clips at least once a year to make sure they are in place. If any are missing, then they should be replaced as soon as possible.

Both of these items are relatively cheap and easy to find. You will typically find the best prices online on sites such as eBay.

If high winds or a storm are forecast then you should make sure that all vents, windows, and doors are shut. Although automatic vents are a wonderful thing, if they open up during a storm it could end up destroying your greenhouse, so turn them off for the duration!

If you live in a particularly windy area, then you may want to consider putting up a windbreak to protect your greenhouse. It may be worthwhile sacrificing some sunshine for protection from the wind.

Siting a greenhouse so the prevailing wind flows over it rather than hits one end is another method of reducing the potential for wind damage.

Another option is to replace your horticultural glass with toughened safety glass. This is stronger so is harder to break. It comes in larger panes so you do not have smaller, overlapping panes. Also, if there is any damage then toughened glass is much easier to clean up than horticultural glass.

Chapter 12: How to grow tomatoes, peppers, tropical fruits, vegetables, fruits, herbs in a greenhouse

Many growers tend to ask the difference between vegetables, herbs, and fruits. A vegetable is a plant or any part of a plant that is considered edible and can be eaten. Herbs, on the other hand, refer to plants or part of plants that are grown as food and also for medicinal purpose while fruits are eatable products containing seeds which are formed from the matured ovary of a flowering plant. The major difference is that while fruits can be referred to as vegetables, vegetables cannot exactly be termed fruits. Also, it is arguable that not all herbs are eaten as the main ingredient as is the case of vegetables.

Growing Vegetables in a Greenhouse

Vegetables are suitable plants to cultivate in a greenhouse because the demand for them is usually high all through the year. However, the vegetables require the right environmental condition for successful cultivation. The grow lights in the greenhouse should be energy efficient and cover the vegetable plantation. During the cold season, the best vegetables to cultivate include; tomatoes, lettuce, spinach, peppers, and cucumbers. But with experience, any kind of vegetable can be successfully cultivated when provided with the right temperature. The key is to maintain a nighttime temperature between 40 – 62°F in the greenhouse depending on the type of vegetable. One of the major issues growers face when it comes to growing vegetables in a greenhouse is the issue of pollination. While some vegetables like tomatoes and peppers can self-pollinate, the others that cannot self-pollinate will require hand pollination. This is achieved by taking the anther of a vegetable and rubbing it carefully against the stigma of another vegetable for a successful transfer of pollen grains. Sometimes, the vegetables that can self-pollinate require being shaken in order to successfully pollinate but a circulation fan can be installed for this purpose.

Vegetables need water but not too much and so it is important not to overwater your greenhouse vegetable garden. A good ventilation system in place will maintain the proper humidity level which will aid the growth of the vegetables in the greenhouse. Using air conditioners in your greenhouse is not the best practice because what conditioners actually do is that they reduce the moisture content in the growing environment. It is advisable to use evaporative air coolers in the greenhouse instead.

Growing Herbs in a Greenhouse

A greenhouse offers the grower the opportunity to be the one in control of the growing environment, this makes it possible and also convenient to grow an herb garden successfully. An adequate supply of moisture is needed for successful cultivation. You may use a sprinkler system with fine hose such that water is supplied in droplets and the proper moisture level of the growing environment is maintained. The most commonly grown herbs in a greenhouse are Chives, Parsley, Basil, Mints, and Chamomile.

Growing Fruits in a Greenhouse

The most popularly grown fruit in a greenhouse is tomatoes, but this does not mean that only tomatoes thrive in a greenhouse environment. All fruits including vines, peaches and even citrus fruits are suitable and can perfectly be grown in a greenhouse environment. Not all varieties of grapevines require high temperature for healthy growth, there are some varieties such as the black Hamburg that grow perfectly in a cool growing environment. The only thing about cultivating vines is that they are attention-demanding as they are susceptible to pest attacks and therefore should be closely monitored in order to ensure a perfect growing condition for them. As the grapevines grow, some maintenance practice needs to be carried out such as spur pruning, fertilization, etc. and waterlogged soil should also be avoided. Peaches and Nectarines are also very suitable for cultivation in a greenhouse but the right variety should be carefully selected. This is because some varieties of Peaches such as Hale's early require the presence of another variety nearby in order to carry out pollination successfully. A suitable variety of Nectarines for greenhouse cultivation is the Pineapple. Hand pollination can be done for the successful pollination of fruits that do not self-pollinate. It is also interesting to know that citrus fruits such as oranges and lemons can be successfully cultivated in the greenhouse.

Chapter 13: Fruit and veg growing calendar

Greenhouses are great for your summer crops and extending your growing season, but if they are heated, you can grow all year long. However, this isn't particularly cost effective as the cost of heating your greenhouse far outweighs the cost of buying the vegetables you can grow.

Saying that though, even an unheated greenhouse helps you to grow throughout the year and can be very cost effective indeed.

In late winter and early spring, you can start off hardy plants such as cabbage, leeks, lettuce, peas, onions, broad beans, Brussels sprouts and so on. These are then planted out once the weather warms up.

If you do heat your greenhouse, then plants such as tomatoes and peppers can be started off early too.

In mid-spring, your more tender plants are started off, such as pumpkins, zucchini (courgettes), squashes, sweetcorn, French beans and so on. This means that towards late spring they are ready to be planted outside or under glass. At this time of year, you can also buy ready grown pepper and tomato plants for your unheated greenhouse.

As spring progresses and summer begins you can plant your summer plants in their final locations in your greenhouse. Your outdoor crops are hardened off and planted out once the risk of frost has passed, which frees up space in your greenhouse.

If you have space in your greenhouse then towards the end of summer you can sow lettuces, salad leaves, and even baby carrots under glass for a later crop. You can also plant your Christmas potatoes in bags.

In winter time you can sow your broad beans and peas to overwinter before being planted out in spring. Calabrese and French beans can be planted and will mature in the greenhouse. Hardy lettuces will also grow happily in your greenhouse. You can also start any over-winter onions too.

Hardy plants such as kale and chard typically grow well outside during the colder months, but in some areas, they may benefit from being under glass during the extreme cold to ensure you get a good crop.

What you can grow throughout the year in your greenhouse will depend greatly on where in the world you live and how cold it gets. In colder areas with heavy snowfall plants which would be left outside over winter (kale, Brussels sprouts, etc.) will benefit from the protection of the greenhouse. If nothing else this will prevent the snow from damaging the plants.

In warmer areas, the greenhouse will let you start your plants off much earlier so you can make the most of the growing season.

Unless you are going to heat your greenhouse, you will not be able to get crops such as tomatoes, cucumbers, peppers and chilies during the winter months. Unfortunately, the cost of heating tends to be prohibitive.

Most greenhouse owners will usually only heat their greenhouse enough to prevent frost, which will damage their tender plants. If you grow rare or unusual plants that cannot tolerate colder temperatures, then heating becomes much more expensive but necessary.

The location of your greenhouse plays a big part in how much you need to heat your greenhouse and what you can grow over the winter months.

A greenhouse positioned in a sunny, sheltered area will obviously remain warmer than one, such as mine, which is located in the open. A lean-to greenhouse will be warmer because it benefits from the heat coming through the wall from the house behind.

When it comes to growing all year long, you can be creative. But with so many variables there are no hard and fast rules, so you will have to experiment, seeing what works best in your greenhouse in your area.

Chapter 14: Hydroponics in a greenhouse

Growers, especially new growers, tend to wonder how true the possibility of growing plants effectively without soil is. Well, it is not only true that it is possible but it is also more popularly practiced than one would usually assume. Growing without soil, which is also called Hydroponics, is a technique of cultivating plants using a prepared nutrient solution.

The idea is based on the fact that all plants generally need only light, air, water, and nutrient to grow healthily. And while the plants grown on soil would struggle to get all these necessities from the soil and the environment, they can be easily provided to them by the grower especially in an enclosed environment such as a greenhouse. The plants can grow anywhere as long as they are supplied with the necessities for their healthy growth.

Hydroponics (growing without soil) is a creative technique that offers people with non-arable lands although interested in gardening the chance to finally have their own garden without having to worry about the poor soil condition in their area because they won't even need to use soil at all.

If you are new to this, you might want to ask how this system works, it is quite simple and we will get right to it now:

How does Hydroponics work?

In this system of gardening, the roots of the plants are dipped inside a nutrient solution contained in a reservoir. The nutrient solution is pre-mixed with all the needed nutrients by the particular plant being cultivated. Using this system makes it easy to plant more in a seemingly limited space in a greenhouse. It also improves the yield at the end of the day, producing healthier products that are free from any form of diseases and pests. There are generally 6 major methods of hydroponic system, these are Aeroponics, Wick Irrigation system, Flood and Drain, Water culture, Nutrient film technique, and Drip system.

Drip system

This is a method of hydroponics which employs the use of drip lines to transfer the nutrient solution directly to the base of the plants regularly. While soil is not used, a growing medium is essential in this method of hydroponics to support the plants. This method is usually used in a large-scale production garden but for it to work effectively, it requires that each plant has its own container and invariably its own drip line. A pump system can be used (with an attached timer for automation) to take water into the drip manifold when needed. The timer is important to avoid flooding the plants and causing more harm than good in the process. A drip system can also be either a recovery system where the excess nutrient solution is recycled or a non-recovery system where the excess nutrient solution is drained off as waste instead.

Nutrient Film Technique

This method of hydroponics is usually used to grow small and quickly growing plants. The growing tray is set at an angle that enables a constant flow of the nutrient solution. The interesting thing about this method of hydroponics is that it doesn't even require a growing medium as the roots of the plants are suspended in the air. The NFT method requires the use of a pump which pumps the nutrient solution into the growing tray and also another pump connected to an air stone to ensure aeration in the nutrient solution.

Water Culture

his method of hydroponics is considered suitable for commercial growers interested in large-scale production because it is cheap. It is a very simple method, if not the simplest of all methods, as the plants are placed in hanging baskets while their roots are suspended in the nutrient solution. Because the roots of the plants are always in the nutrient solution, an air pump is important to supply oxygen for aeration in the reservoir holding the nutrient solution.

Flood and Drain

This method is also called ebb and flow. In this method, the root system of the plants is flooded with nutrient solution intermittently and the supply is usually controlled by a timer. When the timer is off and the pump stops, the nutrient solution flows back down into the reservoir through the overflow tube set as a draining system. A bigger tube should be used as the overflow tube and the grower should also keep in mind that a growing medium is needed to support the roots of the plants in this method of hydroponics.

Wick Irrigation System

The hydroponic wick system is the easiest system to set up because there is no need for electricity or the use of a pump in the system. It's a good choice for growers just starting out with hydroponics although it's not a suitable system for larger plants. The container which holds the plants in this method is placed on the reservoir containing the nutrient solution and a wick is used to suck up the nutrient solution into the growing medium in the container holding the plants.

Aeroponics

This is said to be the most advanced method of hydroponics; it does not require a growing medium as the roots of the plants are merely suspended in the air. The suspended roots are fed by a sprinkling system set up in the nutrient solution and the attached nozzles should be specially designed to deliver the nutrient solution in mist form. It is said that aeroponics gives more yield than other methods of hydroponics, this is probably because aeroponics allows the grower to grow more in a limited space and also because the exposed root system of the plants gives them access to more oxygen and thereby aerates faster and better.

It is important to note that the roots of the plants in aeroponics tend to dry out faster and therefore must be fed with a nutrient solution as often as needed. A timer can be set accordingly to ease up the stress while the grower ensures that there is no power outage or provides a backup power supply in case there is a power failure.

Growing without using soil is best carried out in a greenhouse and while it requires a bit of 'technical know-how', the quality of the result that will be obtained cannot be overemphasized when things are done right.

The right method of hydroponics should be chosen based on the purpose of gardening and the right nutrient solution should be used for the right plant not forgetting the use the right growing medium when the method chosen requires one. All these are important so as to achieve successful soilless cultivation in a greenhouse.

Chapter 15: Greenhouse insect management, pest control and fertilization

Insect management

Solutions to insect problems include insect predators or other predators like you. When you put beer out for slugs, squish aphids with your fingers, or discard an infested plant, you are functioning as a predator. If no other solution works, you can spray. Sometimes simply a strong spray of clear water will wash insects off plants; many bugs are too fragile to survive this.

Showers

Some very successful indoor gardeners give most of their potted plants (not cacti and similar kinds) a weekly shower. They put the pot in the bathtub and turn on tepid water from overhead. This gets rid of many insects before the gardener has even begun to notice them, and the "rain" is good for most plants.

Other Sprays

The next step is a soap spray. You can buy an insecticidal soap solution, or you can put a drop of dishwashing liquid in a gallon of water. Other popular organic sprays involve garlic, onion, hot pepper, or a combination thereof, ground up and mixed with a great deal of water. A certified organic farmer I know makes "nettle tea" by leaving nettles in water in a barrel outdoors "until it stinks to high heaven," then diluting the tea ten to one or more. He recommends it highly; it may smell up your greenhouse, but it will kill many bugs.

Other Organic Poisons

A few years back, rotenone and pyrethrum, or pyrethrins, were all the rage with organic gardeners, including me. Now I never use them. They are organic in the sense that they are made from plants; rotenone is made from the root of a South American plant, and pyrethrum from a variety of chrysanthemum. Unfortunately, both can kill creatures you don't want killed, like spiders and ladybugs, or, in the garden, bees. Rotenone is particularly deadly to fish. You may not keep fish in the greenhouse, although a few greenhousers do, but pesticides have a way of getting into the water table.

Traps

Insect traps are not usually used in the greenhouse, except for one kind. Aphids, whiteflies, and many other undesirables are attracted to bright yellow. You can buy sticky 3-by-5-inch "cards" of this color, or circles of the same material, and set them up as traps. Hundreds of bugs will get stuck on them; when one gets too gross, throw it away and set up another one in the wire holder that comes with it. If you are really thrifty, you can buy a bottle of the sticky stuff, clean dirty traps with cooking oil, and recoat them.

Pest control

Gardeners like you often choose the path of gardening because plants can enjoy optimum growth under greenhouse conditions. However, the moderate warmth and moist also made a greenhouse the perfect nest for most pests. Greenhouses can act as a barrier of protection but pests can always sneak through small gaps. Below are the tips that will help in eradicating pests from your greenhouse

Greenhouse cleaning routine

Just like any other space in your house, you need to have a cleaning routine for your greenhouse. During the summer, you can move all the plants and gardening tools out from your greenhouse so cleaning activities can be carried out. Scrub the walls and floor with hot water and detergent solution. Pay particular attention to the corners and cracks as these are the likely places where pests will lay their eggs.

Freeze your greenhouse

If the environment inside your greenhouse is always warm and nice, pests will love it. It is good if you can freeze your greenhouse during winter season as cold temperature is the best way to kill or get rid of most pests. Before you do this, make sure that you have an alternative storage for your plants. It can be your warehouse, min indoor garden or you can simply freeze them inside the greenhouse. This is because pests might hide themselves and their eggs within the plants. If you have chosen the greenhouse plants that are able to grow without optimum growing conditions provided by the greenhouse, they should be able to be frozen inside the greenhouse. Even so, you should pay particular attention to their growth.

Sterilize gardening tools and soil

Before moving any new gardening tools or gardening materials into your greenhouse, make sure that you have properly sterilized them. Instead of using a normal garden soil, you should opt for a sterilized potting mix that are often pest free. As for your gardening tools, bleach them in a detergent solution. You must be very strict when it comes to this. Most of the time, you only have yourself to blame if your greenhouse suffers a pest infestation because you are the one showing them where the paradise is.

Constantly look out for pests

To prevent a total outbreak of pests, you need to monitor your plants closely. Destroy any eggs, larvae or bugs that you suspect to be harmful to your greenhouse garden. You may want to consider treating a particular plant separately. This is to avoid pests from moving effortlessly to another plant while treatment is being conducted. Do not be lazy because one a pest infestation takes place; it will take a long time for you to get rid of the whole colony because the environment inside the greenhouse provides a great breeding ground for these notorious creatures.

Introduce biological pest control

Consider deploying beneficial insects within your greenhouse. These predatory insects will feed on pests that are present inside your greenhouse in no time. Some of the beneficial insect that you can consider are ladybugs and praying mantis. You can get these from your local nurseries or even order them online. This method is not only organic but it will also save you a lot of time and effort trying to pick up harmful pests while performing your greenhouse gardening chores.

Use potting soil

Often ordinary garden soil will be packed with a lot of insect eggs, creepy crawlies and other pests. Therefore, for the plants inside containers in the greenhouse, its best to use a good potting soil or compost for potting them. The soil should be rich in nutrients, sterilized free from any diseases and pests to help the plants grow.

Practice crop rotation

If you plant directly into the ground in your greenhouses, obviously you will not have much better control over the spread of pests and diseases inside the soil. Crop rotation is a better way to combat this by growing different type of plant in the structure each year. It will discourage the building up of pests in the soil since the same plant usually promotes similar kinds of pests.

Use netting

Greenhouses require proper aeration, and it is not ideal to seal them up absolutely to prevent pests from entering. But you could reduce the number of big flying insects that come in by hanging netting, open windows, or other vent points.

Move pots outside in the heat

In the summer periods, a greenhouse will usually become hot and dry through the day. Taking plants in pots outside will not only help in cooling down the plants but also cut down the buildup of spider mites on them. Spider mites multiply in numbers in warm climates, so the ideal thing is to keep the greenhouse aerated and also use a mister to keep the humidity up. If you are leaving the house for the day, it's ideal to douse the floor of your greenhouse with water, which would evaporate into the air through the rest of the day.

Fertilization

Your greenhouse is the best investment you have ever done in terms of productivity and hobby. You can get a good source of income even from a small greenhouse by growing some vegetables, fruits, or flowers. But remember that greenhouse gardening is not like traditional gardening and you have to do utmost care of your plants for best production. Greenhouse plants need more amount of nutrients than outdoor gardening and you must provide them through proper means. Keeping your soil fertile should be your major concern because many plants die in the absence of proper nutrients. Plants use a process called photosynthesis to produce some major nutrients on their own. So, unlike animals, plants only need some inorganic compounds to produce essential nutrients for their growth. Some of these nutrients like carbon, hydrogen, oxygen, nitrogen, phosphorus, potassium, Sulphur, calcium and magnesium are required in large quantities by plants and hence are called macronutrients. On the other hand, some other elements like iron, manganese, zinc, copper, boron, chlorine, and molybdenum are required in fewer amounts by greenhouse plants and thus called micronutrients.

Plants can take some of the macronutrients naturally through photosynthesis. For example carbon is taken from the air in the form of CO2   through the leaf stomata and fixed into organic compounds via photosynthesis. Plants can extract hydrogen and oxygen from water. Other common nutrients like calcium, magnesium, and sulphate can be extracted from the soil and hence they are not included in the fertilization. So, there are only 3 main macronutrients called sodium, potassium, and nitrogen that your plant needs in the form of fertilizers.

Your greenhouse plants can easily get some major macronutrients from the soil, water, and photosynthesis. But there are still many nutrients that you greenhouse plants need in the form of fertilizers. Here is a list of some common nutrients and their use for your greenhouse plants: --

Nitrogen

Necessary for the generation of leaves and development of stem. It likewise assumes a noteworthy part in building plants cells.

Phosphorus

Required for the advancement of plants and their leafy foods in the development of sound roots.

Potassium

Used by the plants amid photosynthesis and fundamental for its development.

Sulphur

Helps to create vitality for a plant and builds the viability of phosphorus.

Iron

Necessary for the generation of chlorophyll.

Manganese

Aids in the ingestion of nitrogen and a crucial segment in vitality exchange process.

Zinc

Essential part for the vitality transference process.

Copper

Essential for the generation of chlorophyll.

Boron

Required in least sum yet genuine utilization is not yet known.

Magnesium

One of the principle segments of chlorophyll. It is likewise in charge of disseminating phosphorus all through the plant.

Calcium

Helps in root development and the plant to retain potassium.

Chlorine

Necessary for photosynthesis.

Molybdenum

Helps in some chemical reactions of your plant.

Chapter 16: Strategies to avoid insects

The term pest control often conjures up images of people using sprays filled with chemicals. You might think that using such methods is rather extreme. But if you spot your wonderful tomatoes surrounded by ants or your beautiful flowers suddenly attacked by flies, then you might think of drowning those creatures in pesticides.

However, what might sound like a frightening scenario can typically be solved by taking a few precautionary steps. If all else fails and you still would like to consider using sprays, then do not worry.

The thing about pesticides is that they have an instant (and noticeable) effect. You can see the number of pests on your plants reduced. Nevertheless, there are certain effects in the long term – such as depleting the health of your soil and slightly poisoning your water – that might prove disastrous for you in the future. You might have to change the soil entirely. If you are using a raised bed, then this might not be a problem. However, if you have decided to plant directly into the earth, then getting rid of all that pesticide residue is a strenuous process.

Here is another thing that you should keep in mind; sometimes, getting rid of the pests may not be necessary. If you have aphids roaming around on your plants, then see if you have helpful insects that dine on these aphids. In fact, certain farmers are known to let the pests live. This is because they usually have some form of predator that can take care of the pest problem. This has two beneficial results:

- You do not have to spend time (and money, in some situations) on pest control activities.

- You let someone (or something) else take care of the problem for you. A friend in need is a friend indeed. Even if that friend just happens to have four legs, wings, or antennae.

Another thing to keep in mind; your problem might not be related to pests. It is easy to think that certain creatures have wreaked havoc on your lovely garden. Actually, it is certainly tempting to think that way. However, in many cases, the situation might just be because of other factors. Is there enough moisture for the plants? Are strong winds causing harm to them? Was there heavy rainfall recently? Did it hail? Even water pollution could be another factor to consider. You see, all of these factors cause unnecessary stress on the plants, which further begins to attract the pests in your area. Trying to get to the root of the problem might help you effectively remove the pests without using any pest control techniques (including pesticides).

The idea behind evaluating your garden is to know what kind of problem you are dealing with. That may help you decide if you would like to head over to the next step, which is the integrated pest management, or 'IPM' for short, process.

In IPM, farmers and gardeners take gradually stronger steps to get rid of the pests in their garden. They start by working on the conditions that help the growth of the crops. Are these conditions beneficial? Do the crops have everything they need? Once they are able to work around these conditions, they seek to establish a level of damage they can accept. Once that is done, they move on to using methods that have minimal toxicity. If that does not work, they begin using toxic or invasive methods.

Join the Resistance!

The first thing that you should do is focus on creating pest resistance plants. You see, gardeners and farmers often work with a plethora of plants species. Some of these plants have some unique traits. One of those unique traits is the ability of the plant to have disease resistance. This means that the plant suffers minimal damage from a specific disease, similar to how the human immune system builds resistances against diseases.

Many of the modern plants have built resistance to many diseases that could cause considerable damage. What's more, you can find plants that also have resistance to certain insects. For example, you can find special types of squash that can keep away certain types of beetles. This might help you effectively find a solution against these pests without having to resort to other methods of pest control.

In fact, when you are purchasing plants, you might receive information about what pests those plants resist. After knowing what pests are common in your area, you can match the plant to that particular pest.

Inviting Less Pests

While you might be confident that you have taken all the precautionary steps to keep away pests, there might be certain reasons your garden is still attracting those nasty critters.

Mixed Plants

Most insects have receptors that allow them to target their favorite plants. It is how bees can seek out nectar so easily. If you have the plants that insects are waiting to attack and you have done nothing to protect those plants, then you might as well schedule buffet hours for the insects! What you can do to avoid this situation is to plant your crops in small batches throughout your garden. Then you can add other plants into the mix (preferably those that have resistance against the pests in your area). This confuses the insects, tricking them into believing that perhaps your garden does not have the food they are looking for. Additionally, you might be able to avoid diseases from spreading when you mix plant breeds.

Timing

Certain pests often arrive during certain climates. This fact might give you an idea of the kind of threat you are dealing with. When plants are young, they do not have the strength to ward off pests effectively, which is why you can plant your crops early so that by the time pest climate arrives, your crops have strong tissues. In some cases, insects often leave eggs behind in gardens. When the larvae hatch, they find a ready source of food in the plants around them. For this reason, you could also plant your crops a few weeks after the larvae have hatched, allowing you to starve the pests before working on your garden.

Here is a pro tip: speak to farmers in your area about the emergence of pests. They have extensive knowledge about when these pests might come out during a particular season, allowing you to know how long to wait before planting your crops.

Crop Rotation

You can move around the crops to new locations in your greenhouse each year. This does not give pests a particular spot to target. Shifting locations confuses the pests, who might be used to finding plants in a specific spot of the garden. Certain insects often lay their eggs in one location when they realize that they know where they can find a ready supply of food. However, by moving your crops around, larvae that hatch might not find their food source. Before they can discover food, they might starve and you might be able to get rid of them without much effort. Do note that crop rotation is most commonly possible with annual plants, when they can be cycled year after year. Perennial plants are usually harvested after one year, so they cannot be quickly rotated. So make a note of this when you plan to change plant locations in your garden. More on annual and perennial plants in Chapter 10.

Go Easy on the Fertilizer

This might be a common mistake committed by beginners. Gardeners who are starting out might worry about the amount of fertilizer that they use. Many use too much to avoid using too little. Unfortunately, too much fertilizer can cause harm to plants, just the way too little can. In fact, you could say that increasing the amount of fertilizer to a plant is like giving steroids to them! For example, soil nutrients provide nitrogen to the plant. This is good in moderate quantities. By adding more fertilizer, you increase the supply of nitrogen. Providing excess amounts of nitrogen might cause rapid growth in plants. This causes them to end up being juicy. This might not sound all that bad. Who doesn't love juicy food? You and every other multi-legged creature will be waiting to get a bite out of those plants. Pests might become attracted to the unnatural growth, finding a rich source of food for them and their offspring.

Clean Up Other Materials

If you notice fallen leaves, fruits, or other objects in your garden that should not typically be there, then make sure you clear them out. These objects and debris might carry organisms and pests on them that could be transferred to your plants. This increases the chances of infecting your plants with diseases or sending pests into their midst. Once you have cleaned up, see if you can also cultivate the soil when you get the opportunity. This reveals any hidden pest eggs. Additionally, if there are any larvae, you might just let predators (or even the weather) get rid of them.

Make Friends With Creatures

I am not asking you to invite creatures into your house for tea and supper. What I mean is to allow the growth of certain organisms that could help you get rid of pests. For example, certain types of spiders leave your plants alone, but find abundant food in the pests that might live there. You can always encourage the growth of these pest-hunters, as you can call them.

Insecticides

These are a form of pesticide that are specifically made to harm, eliminate, or repel one or more species of insect. You can discover insecticides in various forms such as sprays, gels, and even traps. Pick one based on the pest that is attacking your garden.

Once you have selected your insecticide, it is better to know the below tips:

- I would recommend using just one type of insecticide in your garden. Adding two or more insecticides diminishes their effect and may inadvertently cause harm to your garden.

- Remember that not all insecticides take the same time to remove pests from your garden. You might have to wait longer for certain types.

- Try to see if you really need the spray. For example, if you want to get rid of ants, you could use a bait instead (after all, ants are attracted to nearby sources of food).

Fungicides

These are pesticides that are made to kill fungal infections on the plants and any fungi spores that might have latched onto your crops. In some cases, fungicides are used to mitigate the effects of mildew and mold. The way they function is by damaging either the fungal cell structure or stopping the energy production in cells.

When you are ready to use your fungicide, do make note of the below tips:

- In many cases, people might accidently diagnose fungal diseases for their plants when in reality, it might not be a disease at all. Make sure you use the help of local experts to give you a second opinion. They might just prevent you from buying a fungicide needlessly and might recommend another solution.

- Make sure that leaves are not kept wet for too long. Simply keeping the leaves dry after watering them helps reduce the spread of fungi.

- Keep your tools sanitized. Sometimes, the fungi could spread from one plant to another because they stuck to the tools you were using.

Herbicides

The main purpose of herbicides in a garden is to get rid of all the weeds.

When you have gotten your herbicide, do make note of the following tips:

- Always make sure that the instructions on the herbicide suit your purposes.

- Go easy on its application. Adding more herbicide might sound like a safe bet, but it might end up damaging your plants. If you feel unsure, read the instructions provided on the herbicide to understand its usage quantity.

- Certain herbicides show immediate results. Others take a while to get rid of the weeds. Always check with the seller or supplier for details before using the herbicide. This way, you are not left wondering if you had bought a defective product when you see weeds present even after the third day of using the herbicide.

- Herbicides also have an effect on the soil, so make sure you speak to experts about your garden's soil types before you make a purchase.

Chapter 17: How to clean your greenhouse

Greenhouse cleanliness is absolutely vital. Whether you own a greenhouse, a polytunnel, a cold frame or a portable greenhouse, regular cleaning is vital.

Over time pathogens such as bacteria, pests and fungus will build up in your greenhouse, and these can have a devastating effect on your plants.

When you clean your greenhouse will depend on what you grow in it. If you are only growing plants in the summer months, then you clean your greenhouse in winter, when the crops have all been cleared out.

However, if you grow all year round, then a mild spell in late September or October is the best time to clean. This allows you to put your delicate plants outside while you clean your greenhouse thoroughly. The cleaning also makes sure that your plants get maximum light during the darker winter months.

You will want to put aside a day to clean your greenhouse to ensure you have plenty of time to do the job. Choose a day that is dry and mild, particularly if you are putting tender plants outside.

Firstly, you need to remove your plants from the greenhouse. If you are concerned about them, then cover them with some horticultural fleece to keep them warm.

Then remove any empty pots, the greenhouse staging and as much as you can so the greenhouse is empty.

Your first job is to brush out all the debris from the greenhouse such as soil, fallen leaves and other odds and ends that have been dropped in the growing season. If you have a portable vacuum cleaner, then these are a big timesaver.

Any fallen leaves, particularly from tomatoes and squashes should be destroyed rather than composted.

The internal structure of the greenhouse then needs to be cleaned. Use hot water if you can and try to avoid chemicals which could remain in your greenhouse and harm your plants the following year.

Hydrogen peroxide is a particularly good cleaner that has little impact on the environment. There are specialist greenhouse cleaners on the market and garden disinfectants can be used.

You can use domestic cleaning products, but you need to be careful as these can contain harmful chemicals which can hang around in your greenhouse for months.

Once the structure is clean, then the panes need cleaning. Remove any old shade paint and give them a good scrub both inside and out. Remove any dirt trapped between the panes and, if necessary, remove panes to clean any algae.

Take this time to check the rubber seals and the glass clips on your greenhouse. Any that are perished, broken or missing need to be replaced. Also check all vents, vent controllers, and draught excluders, making good any necessary repairs.

The gutters on your greenhouse need to be cleaned out. Check the downpipes for blockages and remove any debris. Where the gutter meets the downpipe, there should be a wire mesh to prevent debris blocking the pipe. Make sure this is fixed in place properly, though if it is missing you need to buy or make one.

Check that all the gutters are firmly in place and are not leaning as this can lose you precious water.

Over summer your water butts will often gather debris land grow algae or harbor mosquito larvae. Empty out your water butts and give them a good scrub out using non-toxic cleaning products. Rinse the water butt thoroughly before putting back in position. You can add potassium permanganate crystals which turn the water a light pink color. This will help prevent the build-up of algae in the water.

Clean and replace the lids of your water butts as this helps prevent debris from getting into them.

Although dirty water won't harm your grown plants, it can be too much for delicate seedlings and seeds. It can contain pathogens that will harm them so always use tap or municipal water on your delicate plants.

If your greenhouse has a wooden frame, then you need to treat the wood as well. This will prevent the wood from rotting and extend the lifespan of your greenhouse.

Your greenhouse staging should also be cleaned like the rest of your greenhouse. If it is wooden, then treat it with an appropriate preservative to prevent rot or damage to it.

Any pots that are going to be reused should be emptied of compost and cleaned with a good disinfectant. This will prevent the build-up of bacteria and pests.

Once everything is cleaned and treated, then you can put everything back into your greenhouse. Take the opportunity to organize everything to make the best use of space and minimize the potential hiding places for pests looking to overwinter somewhere warm.

Conclusion

Thank you for downloading this book. I hope this book has been fruitful in throwing light about greenhouse gardening. Hopefully, it was simple and useful for getting you started on this venture. For some of you, gardening might be a new undertaking while, for other, more seasoned gardeners, this book is just for additional knowledge.

Gardening can be one of the greatest pleasures in your life so why not do it the right way? All the effort you put in will quite literally bloom with results. As you get started with building your own greenhouse or work on improving the one you already have, you will slowly see the difference. There are so many things you can do in your greenhouse garden. It will just grow better over time and fuel you further to keep working at it. Thank you once again, for purchasing this book. I wish you luck with greenhouse gardening.